SCHIRMER'S LIBRARY OF MUSICAL CLASSICS

Vol. 24

STEPHEN HELLER

Fifty Selected Studies

(From Op. 45, 46 and 47)

For the Piano

Selected and Edited by

LOUIS OESTERLE

ISBN 978-0-7935-7295-3

G. SCHIRMER, Inc.

DISTRIBUTED BY

7777 W. BLUEMOUND RD. P.O. BOX 13819 MILWAUKEE, WI 53213

Fifty Selected Studies by Stephen Heller.

Allegretto con moto. ($\quad$ = 100)

2.

Allegro con spirito. ($\quad$=76)

4.

Andante con moto. ($\quarternote$ = 108)

5.

8

Allegretto poco agitato. (♩= 126)

6.

perdendosi

D. C. ad lib.

Moderato. ($\downarrow$ = 100)

8.

Andantino. (♩=84)

13.

Allegretto. *sempre legato ed egualmente.*

15.

Allegretto.

17.

Allegretto con moto.

18.

Allegro.

19.

poco riten. *pp* a tempo

Allegretto comodo.

20.

Andante quasi allegretto.

21.

Poco maestoso.

23.

Andantino con tenerezza.

25.

Allegretto grazioso.

Allegro di molto.

28.

Allegro veloce.

29.

Allegro con brio.

30.

Allegro assai. ($\bullet$ = 126)

31.

Allegretto moderato. (♩= 106)

33.

Allegretto grazioso. (♩.= 84)

34.

Andante cantabile. (♩ = 96)

36.

Allegretto.(♩.= 80)

40.

Andantino.(♩=108)

41.

Allegro vivace. (♩ = 100)

42.

Allegro vivace.

Allegro non troppo.

Allegro con brio.

46.

Allegretto con moto.

47.

cantabile

Allegro risoluto.

Allegretto.

49.